IN DEFENSE OF OUR COUNTRY:

Survivors of Military Conflict

Survivors: Ordinary People, Extaordinary Circumstances

An Enemy Within:
Overcoming Cancer and Other Life-Threatening Diseases

Danger in the Deep:
Surviving Shark Attacks

Gender Danger:
Survivors of Rape, Human Trafficking, and Honor Killings

In Defense of Our Country:
Survivors of Military Conflict

Lost!
Surviving in the Wilderness

Nature's Wrath:
Surviving Natural Disasters

Never Again:
Survivors of the Holocaust

Students in Danger:
Survivors of School Violence

Survival Skills:
How to Handle Life's Catastrophes

Those Who Remain:
What It Means to Be a Survivor

We Shall All Be Free:
Survivors of Racism

When Danger Hits Home:
Survivors of Domestic Violence

The World Gone Mad:
Surviving Acts of Terrorism

IN DEFENSE
OF OUR
COUNTRY:

Survivors of
Military Conflict

by Sheila Stewart
with Joyce Zoldak

 Mason Crest Publishers

IN DEFENSE OF OUR COUNTRY:
Survivors of Military Conflict

MASON CREST PUBLISHERS INC.
370 Reed Road
Broomall, Pennsylvania 19008
(866)MCP-BOOK (toll free)
www.masoncrest.com

Because the stories in this series are told by real people, in some cases names have been changed to protect the privacy of the individuals.

First Printing
9 8 7 6 5 4 3 2 1

ISBN 978-1-4222-0449-8 (series)
ISBN 978-1-4222-1462-6 (series) (pbk.)
    Library of Congress Cataloging-in-Publication Data

Sheila Stewart
with Joyce Zoldak.
CIP data on file with the Library of Congress

Design by MK Bassett-Harvey.
Produced by Harding House Publishing Service, Inc.
www.hardinghousepages.com
Cover design by Wendy Arakawa.
Printed in The Hashimite Kingdom of Jordan.

CONTENTS

Introduction

Each of us is confronted with challenges and hardships in our daily lives. Some of us, however, have faced extraordinary challenges and severe adversity. Those who have lived—and often thrived—through affliction, illness, pain, tragedy, cruelty, fear, and even near-death experiences are known as survivors. We have much to learn from survivors and much to admire.

Survivors fascinate us. Notice how many books, movies, and television shows focus on individuals facing—and overcoming—extreme situations. *Robinson Crusoe* is probably the earliest example of this, followed by books like the *Swiss Family Robinson*. Even the old comedy *Gilligan's Island* appealed to this fascination, and today we have everything from the Tom Hanks' movie *Castaway* to the hit reality show *Survivor* and the popular TV show *Lost*.

What is it about survivors that appeals so much to us? Perhaps it's the message of hope they give us. These people have endured extreme challenges—and they've overcome them. They're ordinary people who faced extraordinary situations. And if they can do it, just maybe we can too.

This message is an appropriate one for young adults. After all, adolescence is a time of daily challenges. Change is everywhere in their lives, demanding that they adapt and cope with a constantly shifting reality. Their bodies change in response to increasing levels of sex hormones; their thinking processes change as their brains develop, allowing them to think in more abstract ways; their social lives change as new people and peers become more important. Suddenly, they experience the burning need to form their own identities. At the same time, their emotions are labile and unpredictable. The people they were as children may seem to have disappeared beneath the onslaught of new emotions, thoughts, and sensations. Young adults have to deal with every single one of these changes, all at the same time. Like many of the survivors whose stories are told in this series, adolescents' reality is often a frightening, confusing, and unfamiliar place.

Young adults are in crises that are no less real simply because these are crises we all live through (and most of us survive!) Like all survivors, young adults emerge from their crises transformed; they are not the people they were before. Many of them bear scars they will carry with them for life—and yet these scars can be integrated into their new identities. Scars may even become sources of strength.

In this book series, young adults will have opportunities to learn from individuals faced with tremendous struggles. Each individual has her own story, her own set of circumstances and challenges, and her own way of coping and surviving. Whether facing cancer or abuse, terrorism or natural disaster, genocide or school violence, all the survivors who tell their stories in this series have found the ability and will to carry on despite the trauma. They cope, persevere, persist, and live on as a person changed forever by the ordeal and suffering they endured. They offer hope and wisdom to young adults: if these people can do it, so can they!

These books offer a broad perspective on life and its challenges. They will allow young readers to become more self-aware of the demanding and difficult situations in their own lives—while at the same time becoming more compassionate toward those who have gone through the unthinkable traumas that occur in our world.

— Andrew M. Kleiman, M.D.

Chapter One

WAR IN AFRICA

war: *noun. Any active hostility or struggle between living beings; a conflict between opposing forces or principles.*

Francine Niyitegeka lay immersed in the mud of the marshes, heavy under-growth shielding her face from view. She held her child in her arms silently, hardly even breathing. Not far away, she could hear shouts, screams, moans, and raucous laughter. If she was discovered, she would die, hacked apart by machetes or clubbed down with a nail-studded stick, like those she could hear dying in other parts of the marshes.

Suddenly, an old woman hiding near her was pulled out and killed. Then, in a night-mare moment, the foliage concealing Francine was pulled back and she saw the killers, their machetes wet with blood. In seconds, her child had been pulled away from her. She watched him die.

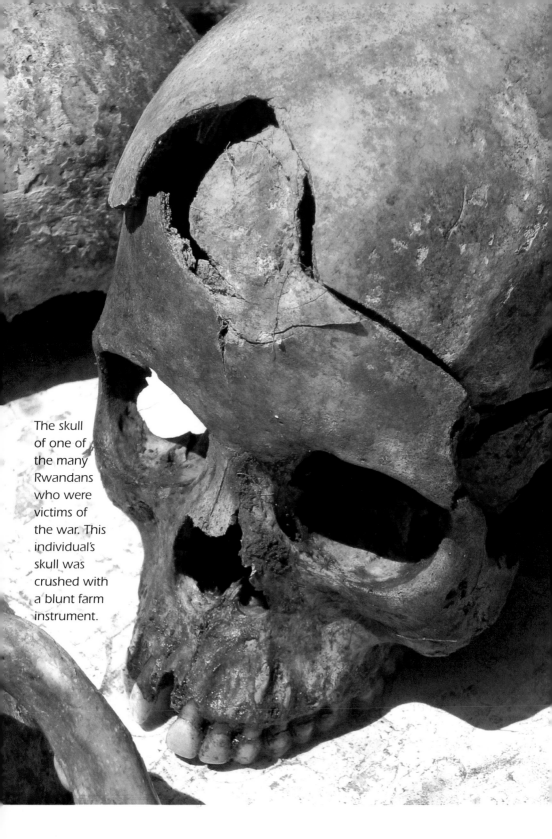

The skull of one of the many Rwandans who were victims of the war. This individual's skull was crushed with a blunt farm instrument.

She found herself begging them not to kill her in the mud of the marshes, to let her die in the grass. The men dragged her out of the mud, and one of them clubbed her in the forehead, knocking her instantly unconscious.

War is always horrible. Innocent people always suffer. Lives are always lost, shattered, changed forever. Even if history were to later agree that the war was relatively necessary, that it had been a "just war," fought in the defense of goodness and the lives of innocents, the war itself is still going to be awful for all the individuals who are caught in its midst.

In recent times, the continent of Africa has perhaps suffered in this way more than any other area. The wars that sweep through parts of Africa are generally civil wars. They begin within one country, and one group rises up against another. The wars are political, with a group trying to take power, seizing control of the government in a **coup**. Sometimes in Africa these groups are **ethnically** based as well, and political parties may then align with a certain ethnic group. Many African countries are very poor, and their governments are not strong. Corruption among the military and among government leaders is common in places where power can be taken by whoever has the most weapons.

The war that raged around Francine Niyitegeka, sending her and thousands of others into hiding in the marshes, took place in Rwanda in 1994. Unrest had been brewing

The root of the English word "war," werra, is Frankish-German, meaning "confusion, discord, or strife," while the verb werran meant "to confuse or perplex."

coup: a successful and unexpected action; often referring to a coup d'etat, a sudden takeover in leadership or power.

ethnically: related to ethnicity, the characterization of groups by background, racial, and cultural traits.

What Is a "Just War"?

Since the days of ancient Greece, philosophers have discussed whether there is such a thing as a just war. Most agree on the following characteristics:

- A just war can only be waged as a last resort. All non-violent options must be exhausted before the use of force can be justified.

- A war is just only if it is waged by a legitimate authority. Even just causes cannot be served by actions taken by individuals or groups who do not constitute an authority sanctioned by whatever the society and outsiders to the society deem legitimate.

- A just war can only be fought to redress a wrong suffered. For example, self-defense against an armed attack is always considered to be a just cause (although the justice of the cause is not sufficient—see point #4). Further, a just war can only be fought with "right" intentions: the only permissible objective of a just war is to redress the injury.

- A war can only be just if it is fought with a reasonable chance of success. Deaths and injury incurred in a hopeless cause are not morally justifiable.

- The ultimate goal of a just war is to re-establish peace. More specifically, the peace established after the war must be preferable to the peace that would have prevailed if the war had not been fought.

- The violence used in the war must be proportional to the injury suffered. States are prohibited from using force not necessary to attain the limited objective of addressing the injury suffered.

- The weapons used in war must discriminate between combatants and non-combatants. Civilians are never permissible targets of war, and every effort must be taken to avoid killing civilians. The deaths of civilians are justified only if they are unavoidable victims of a deliberate attack on a military target.

(*Source*: Vincent Ferraro, professor of international politics, Mt. Holyoke University)

for years between the Hutus and the Tutsis, two ethnic groups in the area. The Tutsis were in the minority, but traditionally had been wealthier and more often held positions of power. In the early twentieth century, Rwanda had been under the control of Belgium. The Europeans upheld—many say established—the Tutsis as the **elite**, and favored them over the Hutus. As a result, resentment simmered among the Hutus.

elite: those people with the highest status and receiving greater privileges and benefits.

But still, most people did not often think about who was Hutu and who was Tutsi. The two groups intermarried and the differences between them were not usually obvious. The Tutsis were taller, many said, with more delicate features. The Tutsis herded cattle, while the Hutus were farmers. But although these descriptions sometimes held true, there was by no means a simple division. In 1931, the Belgians issued identity cards to the Rwandans, with the bearer's ethnicity listed on the card. Today, many Rwandans feel the differences between the Hutus and the Tutsis were manufactured and **exploited** by the Europeans in order to strengthen their own position in the country.

exploited: taken advantage of.

In 1959, the king of Rwanda, a Tutsi, died mysteriously in what many considered an assassination. After this, the tensions between the two groups **escalated**, and many Tutsis fled the country at this time. A few years later, Rwanda gained its independence. Over the next few decades, the tensions simmered, flaring up in conflicts from time to time.

escalated: increased in intensity or amount.

Survivors of Other Wars: The Crimean War

"We now have four miles of beds not 18 inches apart . . . These poor fellows bear the pain of mutilation with an un-shrinking heroism that is really superhuman. . . . I think we have not an average of 3 limbs to a man."
—Florence Nightingale, 5 November 1854

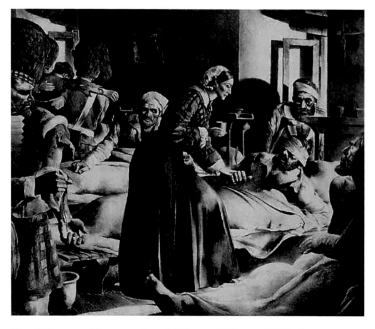

The Crimean War was fought from 1853 to 1856, between Russia on one side and the Ottoman Empire, Great Britain, France, and Sardinia on the other. The cause of the dispute was control of Palestine, a region considered to be holy by many countries. The war was bloody and brutal (as most wars are). Florence Nightingale is shown here tending to the survivors.

By the spring of 1994, the hostility between the Hutus and the Tutus had reached a breaking point. On April 6, the Rwandan president's plane was shot down as it was about to land at the airport in Kigali, Rwanda's capital city. The president had been a Hutu, and the Hutu **militias**, the *interahamwe*, blamed Tutsi **extremists** for the assassination. Later, the Tutsis were to claim that the Hutus had been responsible for the attack, using it as a way to get rid of the president and place the blame on the Tutsis. Truthfully, people did not know for sure who had shot down the president's plane, but the event was enough to send the country spiraling into chaos. Afterward, when people talked of that period, they measured time by the plane crash. Everything began with that.

Before the plane crash, those in Kigali and some of those in the larger towns, had heard the grumblings of unease, the first rumbles of the storm that was to come. On the radio, people denounced the Tutsis, calling them cockroaches. Hutu professors wrote academic papers denouncing the Tutsis. Hutu comedians performed skits calling for the destruction of the Tutsis—so funny even the Tutsis found them hilarious. Hutu musicians wrote catchy songs about killing Tutsis. When a crime was committed against a Tutsi, the authorities did little to catch the perpetrator. The Tutsis had gotten used to living this way. In some areas, though, these rumbles were barely even heard. Life went

militias:
military groups made up of civilians.

extremists:
those who support or use measures beyond the norm on behalf of a cause.

on as usual until the time of the plane crash.

The death of the president seemed to act as a signal to the *interahamwe*. Within hours of the plane crash, the massacre of the Tutsis had begun in Kigali. Although the massacres seemed like madness and chaos at the time, many later commented that they appeared to have been carefully planned. First, those who had disagreed with the president were killed, whether they were Tutsi or Hutu. Soon, Tutsis in general were being slaughtered, no matter their age or position, along with any Hutu who seemed sympathetic to them. In a very short time, the revenge killings had turned to cold-eyed **genocide**; the intent of the killers was to completely wipe out the Tutsi people. "We must finish what we started in 1959!" became one of their rallying cries.

genocide: the purposeful and organized destruction of a certain group of people.

From Kigali, the violence spread quickly. In the towns and villages, Hutu men gathered to listen to groups of *interahamwe* who arrived in trucks. In a book by Jean Hatzfeld called *Machete Season*, one young Hutu, Pancrace Hakizamungili, described what happened on the day the massacres began in his area:

> The first day, a messenger from the municipal judge went house to house summoning us to a meeting right away. There, the judge announced that the reason for the meeting was the killing of every Tutsi without exception. It was

Murambi Technical School in Butari, Rwanda, where over 40,000 people were killed in the genocide of 1994. The buildings now stand as a memorial.

A woman in Rwanda tries to carry on with ordinary life, but it is difficult to recover from the terrible emotional scars left by the war.

simply said, and it was simple to understand.

So the only questions were about the details of the operation. For example, how and when we had to begin, since we were not used to this activity, and where to begin, too, since the Tutsis had run off in all directions. There were even some guys who asked if there were any priorities. The judge answered sternly: "There is no need to ask how to begin. The only worthwhile plan is to start straight ahead into the bush, and right now, without hanging back anymore behind questions."

As soon as the violence began, the RPF—the Tutsi-led Rwandan Patriotic Front, formed from Tutsis who had fled Rwanda—began pushing across the borders from the neighboring countries where they were based, heading for Kigali. It would take them nearly a hundred days to reach the capital and stop the massacres of the Tutsis. In that hundred days, approximately 800,000 Tutsis were murdered, most of them hacked to death with machetes or struck down with clubs.

The Tutsis fled the country when they could; they hid in tiny rooms and in swamps; they ran when they had no other choice, although hiding was better. At first, many tried to take refuge in churches and hospitals, traditional places of sanctuary, but there was no safe place for the Tutsis in Rwanda. The *interahamwe* killed the people in the churches, sometimes defied by the clergy, but sometimes even helped by them. In the hospitals, some Hutu doctors and nurses turned over the refugees to be killed or else killed them themselves.

How did anyone survive such a terrible slaughter? This was war at its worst. War in which the soldiers turned their weapons not on other soldiers but on unarmed innocents, not sparing even tiny children. War in which ordinary men and boys became the soldiers who turned their machetes on their friends and neighbors.

As people died around her, as she found the bodies of her little sisters, of children and neighbors, Berthe Mwanankabandi often wished she were dead. Her story is told in Jean Hatzfeld's *Life Laid Bare: The Survivors in Rwanda Speak:*

> I caught myself asking to die. And yet, I never stood up from my hiding place when I sensed that hunters were nearby. When they were passing, I could no longer command my muscles, which refused to budge. At the last moment, they could not agree to move so that someone would come slit my throat. Just as other people, whom we saw through the foliage, could not hold back one last gesture, raising their arms above their heads to ward off the machete blow that

would kill them outright, even though the ensuing rain of cuts would make them suffer much longer. In our heart of hearts, there crouches a tiny desire for survival that will not listen to anyone.

Hopefully, this Rwandan little girl will grow up in a safer world than her parents did. During war, children are some of the most vulnerable to violence.

The Memorial
Gardens at
the Genocide
Memorial in
Kigali, Rwanda,
are a statement
of hope for the
future.

Many survived through luck. The *interahamwe* did not look in their particular hiding place, or failed to come back and finish the job. The *interahamwe* killed Tutsis every day as if it was their job. They began at nine-thirty every morning and kept on until four in the afternoon when the whistle blew to tell them they could stop. Some were saved by this whistle at the last minute as the Hutu men suddenly turned away and headed back to the villages to wash the blood from their arms and eat supper.

More than just surviving the actual slaughter, though, how could anyone survive afterward? Many of the Tutsi survivors bear scars from machete blows, some are missing limbs, and all of them have been wounded emotionally. They saw their families and friends cut down around them. They saw the faces of their killers, faces they knew well, faces they remembered laughing with them in better times. How could they ever trust anyone again?

IMMACULÉE ILIBAGIZA

In 1994, Immaculée Ilibagiza, a Tutsi university student, was standing on a hill near her village when she heard screams. She looked toward the sound and saw, on the hill opposite her, someone being killed with a machete. She was stunned and shocked; never had she seen such a thing before. Quickly, her father told her to run, to go to the minister's house three miles away and plead with him to hide her. The minister was a Hutu, but he had always been kind to her family.

While many Hutus turned their backs on their Tutsi friends, this minister pulled Immaculée inside and led her to a tiny bathroom at the back of the house. Although the room was only three feet by four feet, six Tutsi women were already huddled there. Immaculée squeezed inside and the minister shut the door behind her.

For the next three months, the seven women lived in the tiny room, fearing at every moment that they would be discovered

The old Rwandan flag was associated with the genocide, so this new flag was adopted in 2001. The blue band represents happiness and peace, the yellow band symbolizes economic development, and the green band symbolizes the hope of prosperity. The sun represents enlightenment.

and killed. The bathroom was so small that they had to take turns sitting and standing. They could not speak above a whisper for fear they would be heard. They could not bathe or brush their teeth. They could only flush the toilet if someone in another bathroom flushed the toilet at the same time, so the sound would not alert the ever-present *interahamwe*.

The Hutus were suspicious of the minister. Several people had seen Immaculée and the others arrive, but no one had seen them leave. Again and again, they searched the house. Once, Immaculée heard someone calling her name.

"Immaculée!" the man shouted. "Come out, Immaculée! I have killed three hundred and ninety-nine cockroaches; I want you to be the four hundredth!"

After ninety-one days in the tiny room, the women, listening to the minister's radio in another part of the house, heard the news that French troops had arrived in Rwanda and had set up a camp nearby to protect Tutsis. Immaculée convinced the minister to help them sneak out of the house and make for the camp. After months in the bathroom, Immaculée had lost forty pounds and her muscles had **atrophied**, but she and the other women managed to walk and then run to the camp.

atrophied: wasted away or decreased in size due to disease or lack of use.

Immaculée later learned that of the Tutsis who had been in her village when the massacres began, she was the only survivor. Her parents and two of her brothers had both been killed in the genocide.

Instead of bitterness, Immaculée has used her experience to reach out to others. She has written a book, called *Left to Tell*, about what happened to her during the genocide. She has set up a fund to provide for children left orphaned by the massacres, and she speaks regularly about peace and forgiveness and the importance of remembering what happened in Rwanda.

What she experienced could have crushed her. She could have let the deaths of her family, of so many people, eat away at her. Instead, she has forgiven those who committed the murders, and she refuses to ever

Rwanda's peaceful green tea fields seem far removed from the violence this nation has seen. Tea is Rwanda's number-one export.

seek revenge. "I don't want it," she told Bob Simon of 60 Minutes. "I don't want them after killing my family to give me this luggage in my heart, in my belly, you know, to hold this anger."

CASSIUS NIYONSABA

Cassius Niyonsaba was only a little boy when the genocide took place. Several years later, when he was twelve, he told Jean Hatzfeld, a French journalist, what he remembered about the genocide. His life before the killings was a haze; he no longer remembered how many brothers and sisters he had had, only that he was the only one left alive. "Because my memory is too taken up by so many deaths, it's not handy with numbers anymore . . . ," he told Hatzfeld. "But I can relive in full transparency the massacres in the church and the ferociousness of the *interahamwe*."

When Hutus started killing Tutsis in his area, Cassius went with his older sister and hid in the local church with many others. After two days, the Hutu killers arrived:

It was not yet noon when the *interahamwe* arrived singing: they threw grenades, they tore down the railings, then they rushed into the church and started slicing people up with machetes and spears. They wore manioc leaves in their hair, they shouted full force, laughed with all their heart. They struck with swinging arms. They cut anyone, without choosing.

People not streaming with their own blood were streaming with the blood of others, oh it was something. So, then, they started dying without resisting anymore. There was a huge uproar and a huge silence at the same time.

In the confusion and horror of the church, Cassius was hit with a hammer and knocked

From the Killers' Perspective: Pio Mutungirehe

"We no longer saw a human being when we turned up a Tutsi in the swamps. I mean a person like us, sharing similar thoughts and feelings. The hunt was savage, the hunters savage, the prey was savage—savagery took over the mind.

"Not only had we become criminals, we had become a ferocious species in a barbarian world. This truth is not believable to someone who has not lived it in his muscles. Our daily life was unnatural and bloody, and that suited us.

"For my part, I offer you an explanation: it is as if I had let another individual take on my own living appearance, and the habits of my heart, without a single pang in my soul. This killer was indeed me, as to the offense he committed and the blood he shed, but he is a stranger to me in his ferocity. I admit and recognize my obedience at that time, my victims, my fault, but I fail to recognize the wickedness of the one who raced through the marshes on my legs, carrying my machete. That wickedness seems to belong to another self with a heavy heart. The most serious changes in my body were my invisible parts, such as the soul or the feelings that go with it. Therefore I alone do not recognize myself in that man. But perhaps someone outside this situation, like you, cannot have an inkling of that strangeness of mind."

(Source: Machete Season, by Jean Hatzfeld)

down. He was still conscious, however, and managed to crawl out of the way. In the evening, when the killers had gone home for the day, Cassius and the other survivors escaped into the forest.

The *interahamwe* came looking for them, of course. They brought dogs to sniff out the Tutsis in their hiding places. Cassius was caught, dragged out into the open, and hit on the head with a machete. He fell, unconscious, and the killers moved on. "At first I ought to have been dead," Cassius said later, "then I insisted on living, but I don't remember how."

A woman found him and carried him away. She hid him under some trees, bandaged his head, and gave him food and water. She was a Tutsi as well, but her husband was a Hutu administrator and this gave her some protection for a while. When her husband discovered she had been helping a Tutsi boy, though, he killed her himself.

The rest of the genocide was a blur to Cassius. He was very sick for a long time, from malaria and from an infection in the machete wound on his head. When the killings stopped, he went home, but everyone was dead.

He went to stay with his Aunt Thérèse, one of the few members of his family still alive. Other children came to live there too, children who also had nowhere to go. Over and over, the children talk about their experiences in the genocide, telling the same stories again and again. "Talking together clears away pain and sadness," Cassius said.

Since the genocide, Cassius has started school again. He watches his aunt's goats, he plays soccer with his friends. But still, he tries to make sense of what happened. The church where he hid with his sister has since been turned into a memorial. Rows of skulls sit on shelves, piles of bones are jumbled together. Many of the survivors cannot bear to even look at the church, and when they must walk past it they hurry by with their eyes downcast. Cassius, though, likes to spend time there:

I look at the holes in the wall every day. I go over to the niches to look at

This child in Rwanda still faces a world filled with many problems. Poverty and AIDS have taken their toll a nation that already bears deep scars.

the skulls, the bones that used to be all those people killed around me.

At the beginning, I felt inclined to cry, seeing those skulls without names or eyes, looking at me. But little by little you get used to it. I sit there for a long time, and my thoughts go off with all of them. I try not to imagine personal faces when I look at the skulls, because if I happen to think about someone I know, then fear grabs me. I simply travel in memory among all those dead who were scattered around and didn't get buried. The sight and smell of the bones hurt me and at the same time, they comfort my mind. They stir up my thoughts, anyway.

Cassius is troubled by what he has learned about people. "At the church," he said, "I saw how savagery can replace kindness in the heart of a man, faster than a driving rain. Now that painful anxiety upsets me." Like so many of the other survivors of the genocide, he cannot find a satisfactory explanation for *why*. There is no good answer for the question.

When he grows up, Cassius wants to become a teacher. "Because," he says, "in school I can take comfort from other people, and because Papa was a teacher."

FRANCINE'S STORY

And what happened to Francine Niyitegeka? When the *interahamwe* clubbed her unconscious, they left her without finishing the job. This was not uncommon during the genocide. Often, the *interahamwe* had so many to kill that they would incapacitate the Tutsis they found, either by knocking them unconscious, as with Francine, or by cutting off their arms and legs so they could not get away. Then, they would come back later, when they had more time, and finish the killing. With Francine, they forgot to come back. She lay, feverish and close to death, for a long time, until her fiancé and a group of other Tutsis found her and rescued her.

When the soldiers of the RPF came to the edges of the marshes and shouted to come out, that they were now free and the genocide was over, the Tutsis in hiding had difficulty

Children Who Kill

In the Rwandan genocides, a number of the killers were young boys, wielding machetes and clubs as though it was a game. "Children as young as ten years old were given machetes and told to do their duty, which sometimes meant murdering their former playmates," writes Bishop John Rucyahana.

In some parts of Africa, rebel groups kidnap children and force them to kill their own families, thus traumatizing, confusing, and isolating them. The children become trained killers, who, because of their youth and innocence, have few defenses against the evil brought against them. One former child soldier, Ishmael Beah, wrote about his experiences in Sierra Leone in his book, *A Long Way Gone: Memoirs of a Boy Soldier.*

Survivors of Other Wars: World War I

"The sky rained shells. . . . Shrapnel was bursting not much more than face high, and the liquid mud from ground shells was going up in clouds and coming down in rain. . . . The dead and wounded were piled on each others' backs, and the second wave, coming up behind and being compelled to cluster like a flock of sheep, were knocked over in their tracks and lay in heaving mounds. The wounded tried to mark their places, so as to be found by stretcher-bearers, by sticking their bayonets into the ground, thus leaving their rifles upright with the butts pointing at the sky. There was a forest of rifles until they were uprooted by shell-bursts or knocked down by bullets like so many skittles.

"The mud which was our enemy was also our friend. But for the mud none of us would have survived. A shell burrowed some way before it exploded and that considerably decreased its killing power.

"Nothing had stood up and lived on the space of ground between ourselves and the pill-box a hundred and fifty yards away. I saw a stretcher-bearer, his face a mask of blood, bending over a living corpse. He shouted to somebody and beckoned, and on the instant he crumpled and fell and went to meet his God."

Soldiers in a battle during World War I. The First World War introduced new and deadlier techniques of warfare.

From the Killers' Perspective: Alphonse Hitiyaremye

"In my dreams I revisit scenes of bloody hunting and looting. Sometimes, though, it is actually me who gets the machete blow and wakes up shaking. He wants to cut me and bleed me out. I try to see who is striking me, but my fear hides the face of the man who wishes me harm. I do not know if he is Hutu or Tutsi, a neighbor or an *inkotanyi* [one of the RPF soldiers]. I would like to know if he is a victim, to ask pardon of his family and hope for peace of mind that way, but the sleeping man refuses."

(*Source: Machete Season*, by Jean Hatzfeld)

believing this to be true. They had heard so many lies from the *interahamwe* during the killings. How could they be sure this was not just another trick? They had heard the *interahamwe* shout reassurances like these, calling for the Tutsis to come out, but those who stood up from their hiding places had been cut down immediately. Finally, the RPF soldiers went and found a boy from the village to confirm their story.

Like so many of the survivors, Francine cannot make sense out of the genocide:

What the Hutus did, it's more than wickedness, more than punishment, more than savagery. I don't know how to be more precise, because although you can discuss an extermination, you cannot explain it in an acceptable way, even among those who lived through it. New questions always come at you out of nowhere.

Survivors of Other Wars: The Civil War

"War is cruelty. There is no use trying to reform it. The crueler it is, the sooner it will be over. . . . It's just like shooting squirrels, only these squirrels have guns."
—instructions to new Civil War recruits

A journalist's sketch made during the American Civil War shows the dead left after a battle.

IS FORGIVENESS POSSIBLE?

The genocide in Rwanda was so horrifying, the killings so atrocious, that the magnitude is difficult to grasp, even for those who lived through it. "Even among ourselves," Cassius Niyonsaba said, "we are startled to hear of the killings we weren't there for, as they're told to us by friends, because the real truth about the killings of Tutsis—it's too much for one and all of us alike." The killers themselves, even during the genocide, also had trouble grasping what was going on: "After the killing we started to feel bad when we heard on the radio about the genocide and how many had been killed," one man later told Anglican Bishop John Rucyahana, "but when we killed, it was like we weren't ourselves. We didn't think about anything except the killing."

When the people involved have trouble even grasping what went on in Rwanda, forgiveness becomes a difficult question. For those in jail for the killings, forgiveness is something they talk about a lot, although they don't know if they should expect it. One of these men, Pio Mutungirehe, told Jean Hatzfeld,

> I can't imagine any forgiveness capable of drying up all this spilled blood. I see only God to forgive me—it's why I ask that of Him every day. Offering Him all my sincerity, without hiding any of my

Survivors of Other Wars: The Russo-Japanese War

The sight was beyond words terrible . . . line after line of Japanese came smiling up to the trenches to be mown down by bullets, until the trenches were full of bodies, and then more came over the bodies of the dead. An officer who was in the fort . . . went mad from the sheer horror of the thing."

—Maurice Baring, survivor of the Russo-Japanese War, 1904

A Japanese painting portrays the violence of Japan's invasion of Russia.

misdeeds from Him. I don't know if He says yes or no, but I do know that I ask Him very personally.

The survivors have various views of forgiveness. For some, like Immaculée Ilibagiza, forgiveness is necessary. For others

Survivors of Other Wars: The Mexican Revolution

"Then Colonel Pablo Lopez . . . said, 'If you want to see some fun, watch us kill these gringos. Come on, boys," he shouted to his followers. . . . I heard a volley of rifle-shots. . . . Colonel Lopez selected two of his soldiers as executioners. . . . One would shoot his victim and then the other soldier would take the next in line. Within a few moments the executioners had gone completely down the line."

—employee of the Cusi Mining Company, survivor of the Mexican Revolution, 1916

A Mexican artist's portrayal of the Mexican Revolution's death and violence.

it is unthinkable, or even meaningless. Cassius Niyonsaba wishes for revenge: "When I think about those who cut Papa and Mama, and all my kin, I'd like them to be shot, so as to draw my thoughts away from my family's miserable end." Janvier Munyaneza feels nothing but sadness. To him, the killers are a faceless mob that he cannot hate. Francine Niyitegeka does not see how forgiveness is possible, or even relevant:

Sometimes, when I sit alone on a chair on my veranda, I imagine a possibility. If, on some distant day, a local man comes slowly up to me and says, "*Bonjour*, Francine. *Bonjour* to your family. I have come to speak to you. So here it is: I am the one who cut your mama and your little sisters," or "I am the one who tried to kill you in the swamp, and I want to ask for your forgiveness," then, to that particular person, I could reply nothing good. A man, if he has drunk one Primus beer too many and he beats his wife, he can ask to be forgiven. But if he has worked at killing for a whole month, even on Sundays, how can he hope for pardon?

Édith Uwanyiligira, sees forgiveness not as a pardoning of the killers, but as necessary for her own healing:

I myself am ready to forgive. It is not denial of the harm they did, not a betrayal of the Tutsis, not an easy way out. It is so that I will not suffer my whole life long asking myself why they tried to cut me. I do not want to live in remorse and fear from being Tutsi. If I do not forgive them, it is I alone who suffers and frets and cannot sleep. I yearn for peace in my body. I really must find tranquility. I have to sweep fear far away from me, even if I do not believe the soothing words of others.

COPING WITH THE PAST

Whether or not the survivors of the genocide can forgive the killers, they must still find some way of dealing with their experiences. Because their horror was so overwhelming, their trauma so deep, their healing comes slowly, a process that for some takes many years.

Some survivors heal by trying to find meaning in their experience and a way to turn their pain to good for the world. One of these survivors is Vital Akimana. Vital was only nine years old when Rwanda erupted in violence. His family fled and, despite many close calls, most of them survived. Today, Vital speaks to groups about his experiences. At Brown University, he told a group of students,

Many people lost their lives, but their existence will not go unremembered. At some point or another we all have our share in contributing to the greed, arrogance and corrupt power that result in the destruction of life. . . . Let's not perpetuate the violence by sharing in

Survivors of Other Wars: World War I

"One of the biggest curses was flies. Millions and millions of flies. The whole side of the trench used to be one black swarming mass. . . . They were all around your mouth and on any cuts or sores that you'd got, which then turned septic. Immediately you bared any part of your body you were smothered."

—Private Harold Boughton of the London Regiment, trenches at Gallipoli, 1915

Soldiers in the trenches at Gallipoli during World War I. The Allies had hoped to find a sea route to Russia, to break the stalemate that stretched across Europe. They landed on Turkey's Gallipoli Peninsula—but war there went no better than in Europe. The Turks poured artillery fire down on the Allies; both sides stared at each other from trenches; and finally, the Allies withdrew. Casualties were high: 252,000 for the Allies and 300,000 for the Turks.

demonize:
to represent as
evil.

victimize: to
make into a
victim.

stories that [are] meant to **demonize** one group and **victimize** another. Let's take part in holding ourselves accountable for our ignorance.

For some, the pain and the scars are so overwhelming that healing, both physically and emotionally, is difficult.

Odette Mupenzi was seventeen years old in 1994 and wanted to become a doctor. When the *interahamwe* broke into the room where her family was hiding, she saw them hack her father to death in front of her. Then one of the men shot her in the face and left her for dead. Her lower face and jaw were destroyed in the attack, but somehow she survived. She was in constant pain, however, and suffered from infections. By 2006, Odette was still living in misery. She could not eat well, her wounds were infected, and she faced almost certain death. When BBC News interviewed her, she told them, "I can't forgive the people that did this to me. It is impossible. . . . I don't have many dreams. I used to dream but I never got to achieve any of the things I had wanted to." At several times, charitable groups had offered to pay for reconstructive surgery for Odette, but the money always ran out before the surgeries could be performed.

Shortly after Odette's interview with BBC News, the Aegis Trust group paid for her surgery out of a fund set up for that purpose. Doctors rebuilt the lower half of Odette's face, using metal rods and skin from her side. In

Survivors of Other Wars: World War I

"Shells from our barrage screeched just over our heads. The enemy artillery, taken by surprise, had not yet opened fire. I set a steady walking pace, everything going according to plan. But after a few steps, I found myself in a huddle on the ground, gasping for breath, bewildered. The blast of a shell had thrown me down violently. As I struggled to get up, to regain balance, still confused, I realised that what seemed to be an unrecognisable heap on the ground alongside me was, in fact, a man. . . . I saw the flash of a rifle: so we could expect some resistance. Another rifle flash, this one straight in front . . . a knock-out blow . . . legs sagging . . . collapse: and as I crossed the hazy limits of consciousness into the non-world, I knew I had been shot through the head."

—Bernard Martin, British lieutenant in World War I, 1917

Survivors of Other Wars: The American Civil War

"In the shadow cast by a tiny farmhouse, sixteen by twenty, . . . lay wearied staff officers and tired reporters. . . . [listening to] the singing of a bird, which had a nest in a peach tree within the tiny yard of the whitewashed cottage. In the midst of its warbling, a shell screamed over the house, instantly followed by another and another. . . .

"[But] who can write the history of a battle when his eyes are immovable fastened upon a central figure of transcendingly absorbing interest—the dead body of an oldest born, crushed by a shell . . . abandoned to death in a building where surgeons dared not to stay?"
—Samuel Wilkinson; sent to cover the Battle of Gettysburg for the *New York Times*, he found the body of his oldest son among the 40,000 who died there.

Boys as young as twelve fought (and died) in America's Civil War.

2008, Odette wrote that she felt alive again. The surgery had saved her life in more ways than one.

The government of Rwanda wants to make sure their country never experiences such division, hatred, and killings again. Tutsis and Hutus now share power in the government. The identification cards, which were sometimes the only way to be sure of a person's ethnic background, are no longer in use. It is now illegal to ask whether a person is a Hutu or a Tutsi. The focus now is on Rwanda, a Rwanda united and thriving.

Rwanda may have learned its lesson—but wars still rip through the rest of Africa, as well as the rest of the world. No country is too great, too civilized, too wise, or too powerful to be immune to the deadly disease called war.

Chapter Two

WAR IN SOUTHEAST ASIA

As a child in Cambodia, Loung was a happy little scamp. She lay on her belly to study bugs crawling across the ground; she tagged after her older brothers, teasing them when they flirted with girls; she stroked frogs' smooth skin; and she never stopped asking questions. Some of her family thought she was a little trouble-maker, but her father told her she was clever. He loved her curiosity.

But when Loung was five years old, her entire world changed. Her father had been a member of the Cambodian Royal Secret Service, but when the Khmer Rouge overthrew the country's government, Loung's family went into hiding. They gave up their nice home, and pretended to be poor, uneducated peasants. Her father became a packer at the

Survivors of Other Wars: The Second Sino-Japanese War

"Those in the first row were beheaded, those in the second row were forced to dump the severed bodies into the river before they themselves were beheaded. The killing went on non-stop, from morning until night, but they were only able to kill 2,000 persons in this way. The next day, tired of killing in this fashion, they set up machine guns. Two of them raked a cross-fire at the lined-up prisoners. Rat-tat-tat-tat. Triggers were pulled. The prisoners fled into the water, but no one was able to make it to the other shore."

—Yukio Omata, Japanese journalist, survivor of the Japanese invasion of China, 1937

A baby cries in terror amid the rubble left by Japan's invasion of Shanghai in 1937. The Second Sino-Japanese War was fought between the Republic of China and the Empire of Japan before and during World War II. It was the largest Asian war in the twentieth century.

port, and her mother now sold old clothes at the market. Loung learned that to talk to strangers could mean danger for her family. "At five years old," she wrote years later, "I am beginning to know what loneliness feels like, silent and alone and suspecting that everyone wants to hurt me."

Disguised as peasants, the family traveled by foot from one village to another. For the next three years, they foraged for their meals in rice fields and garbage; every day they were hungry. Loung's fourteen-year-old sister Keav died of food poisoning.

And then soldiers came and took away Loung's father, the one who had always loved

Skulls from a mass grave of Khmer Rouge victims are stacked up in the Killing Fields near Phnom Penh, Cambodia.

"War
seems to be
ingrained
in human
nature."
—Emanuel
Kant

her best. She never saw him again. Next the soldiers took her mother and her little sister Geak. Now there were only five left of the nine members of Loung's family.

When Loung was eight, she was separated from the rest of her siblings and placed in a child-soldier's camp. There she was taught to use weapons. She became a fierce little wild animal, filled with hatred and rage. She was constantly sick and hungry, and one by one her friends died. When she was nine, a soldier tried to rape her, but she kicked and fought—and got away.

That same year, Vietnamese troops defeated the Khmer Rouge army, and Loung rejoined her siblings. Her older brother Meng and his wife took her with them to America, where they settled in Vermont. Nightmares still haunted Loung's sleep, and she had little in common with the children with whom she now attended school. But at least she was safe. She had survived.

"You can no
more win a
war than you
can win an
earthquake."
—Jeanette
Rankin

Dan Smith also survived the military conflict in Southeast Asia. Unlike Loung, however, the green moist fields of Southeast Asia were not his home; the American army sent him there to serve his country.

Dan grew up on a farm in Illinois. He loved his parents and his little sister; he liked playing basketball and going for long walks with his dog; and he and his girlfriend spent long afternoons making out while they listened to the Grateful Dead and Jefferson

Survivors of Other Wars: The Spanish Civil War

"As we watched, came a sudden egg-dropping explosion of bombs, and ahead, [the village], silhouetted against hills a half mile away, disappeared in a brick-dust-colored cloud of smoke. We made our way through the town, the main street blocked by broken houses and a smashed water main, and stopping, tried to get a policeman to shoot a wounded horse, but the owner thought it was still possibly worth saving. . . .

"A carnival of treachery and rotten-ness on both sides."

—Ernest Hemingway, author, survivor of the Spanish Civil War, 1938

Author Ernest Hemingway was a journalist who traveled to Spain in 1937 to cover the civil war that was going on there. This war had begun when Francisco Franco rose up against an elected, leftist Republican government and ousted it, fighting against the Spaniards who backed that government. The war left an estimated half a million people dead, with both sides committing atrocities against civilians.

Airplane. Life seemed simple and good; he planned to take over his father's farm when he got older, but in the meantime, he was just having a good time. When the letter came that said he'd been drafted, he wasn't happy about it, but most of his friends were going off to Vietnam too. Dan figured he would get it out of the way, and then get on with his life.

Khmer Rouge soldiers tortured their Cambodian victims at this prison in Phnom Penh.

When Dan arrived in Vietnam he was eighteen years old. For the next four years, he would crawl through swamps, his skin constantly damp, itching from mosquito and

The Vietnam War

From 1946 until 1954, the Vietnamese had struggled for their independence from France during the First Indochina War. At the end of this war, the country was temporarily divided into North and South Vietnam. North Vietnam came under the control of the Vietnamese Communists who had opposed France and who aimed for a unified Vietnam under Communist rule, while the Vietnamese who had collaborated with the French controlled the South. In 1965, in an effort to halt the spread of communism, the United States sent in troops to prevent the South Vietnamese government from collapsing. Ultimately, however, the United States failed to achieve its goal, and in 1975 Vietnam was reunified under Communist control; in 1976 it officially became the Socialist Republic of Vietnam. During the conflict, approximately 3 to 4 million Vietnamese on both sides were killed, in addition to another 1.5 to 2 million Lao and Cambodians who were drawn into the war. The Vietnam War was the longest military conflict in U.S. history. The hostilities in Vietnam, Laos, and Cambodia claimed the lives of more than 58,000 Americans, while another 304,000 were wounded.

ant bites; he would eat rats and snakes; he would watch his friends die; and he would kill. The boy he had once been would disappear forever.

Dan came home to a country that was embarrassed by what its armed forces had

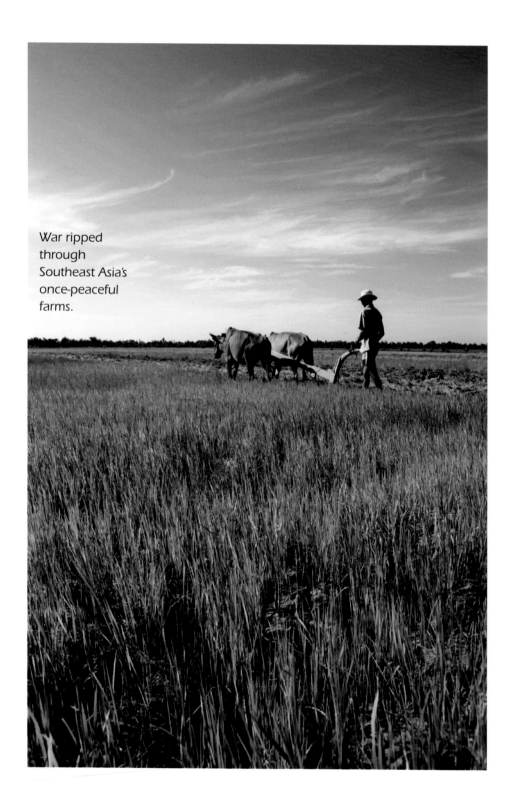

War ripped through Southeast Asia's once-peaceful farms.

done in Southeast Asia. He didn't know how to talk to his parents and sister anymore; his girlfriend had married someone else. "I was like a stranger in my own home," he said. "The only ones who understood me now were other vets. We all had **post-traumatic stress**. Every guy who'd been there had it, some more, some less. We had survived the killing, but we'd didn't fit in 'normal' society anymore. We'd been trained to deal with constant danger, to kill, to stick together— but what good was that back home? We didn't know how to hold a job. Loud noises made us jump. We were always a hair's edge from violence. We'd been taught to have fast reflexes, to shoot quick. That's why we'd survived. But that didn't do us much good when the loud noise was a truck backfiring or someone dropping a book. You ended up sweating, screaming, looking like an idiot over nothing."

post-traumatic stress: an anxiety disorder brought on by traumatic events, often causing nightmares, flashbacks, and social impairment.

LOUNG TODAY

When the war in Southeast Asia was finally over, Loung was able to see the rest of her family who had survived. She went to college in the United States, got married, and took a job at a domestic violence shelter in Maine, where she worked with women who had suffered abuse. In 1997, she became an **activist** on behalf of the Campaign for a Landmine-Free World (CLFW). She used her

activist: one who believes in direct action to oppose or support a cause.

During the Vietnam War, U.S. forces dumped chemicals on the forests that would make the trees shed their leaves, allowing the American military to better see their enemies. These chemicals left yet another war wound, both on the land of Vietnam and the people who were exposed to the chemicals, including U.S. soldiers. The chemicals caused a variety of diseases, including cancer and birth defects.

own story to move listeners to take action for a safer world. In 2001, Loung Ung's story became a bestselling book, *First They Killed My Father*.

But Loung still has nightmares about her past. She's driven to never stop working to build a more peaceful world, but she gets exhausted. "I just started feeling really burned out," she said. "I traveled a ton, but it's the kind of traveling where you go the

Survivors of Other Wars: World War II

"Suddenly I saw people . . . right in front of me. They scream and gesticulate with their hands, and then—to my utter horror and amazement—I see how one after another they simply let themselves drop to the ground. . . . Today, I know that these unfortunate people were the victims of lack of oxygen. They fainted and then burst into cinders. . . . Insane fear grips me and from then on I repeat one simple sentence to myself continuously: 'I don't want to burn to death—no, no burning—I don't want to burn!' . . . I must have stumbled forwards roughly ten paces when I all at once inhaled fresh air. . . . Dead, dead, dead everywhere. Some completely black like charcoal. Others completely untouched, lying as they were asleep. Women in aprons, women with children sitting in trams as if they had just nodded off."

—Margaret Freyer, survivor of the bombing of Dresden during World War II, 1945

In February 1945, the Allied forces bombed the German city of Dresden, killing 600,000 or more civilians. Here officials inspect the dead after the bombing was over.

Survivors of Other Wars: World War II

"I picked my way over corpse after corpse in the gloom, until I heard one voice raised above the gentle undulating moaning. I found a girl, she was a living skeleton, impossible to gauge her age, for she had practically no hair left, and her face was only a yellow parchment sheet with two holes in it for eyes. She was stretching out her stick of an arm and gasping . . . , 'English, English, medicine, medicine,' and she was trying to cry, but she didn't have enough strength. And beyond her down the passage in the hut there were the convulsive movements of dying people too weak to raise themselves from the floor."

—Richard Dimbleby, BBC reporter, entering the Belsen concentration camp a few days after liberation by the Allied soldiers, 1945

A mass grave at the Belsen concentration camp. The Allied liberators were horrified to find how many human beings had not survived this war's terrible violence.

night before . . . and then the next morning you fly out, and you're exhausted." But Loung feels she can't say no to opportunities where she can speak out against war. "People who went through [war], people who lived through it, don't get a break because they're exhausted."

Loung wants young people to know: "Peace isn't free and it isn't automatic. It requires commitment. It requires strategy. It requires work. What we do totally matters. My story is an illustration of that—it's a testimony. I actually was living on the street, eating out of garbage cans, and somebody, somewhere, realized that peace is not an automatic and that changing the world takes work and action. . . . They got out of their comfort zones, they picked up a phone, they traveled to Asia, they sent blankets, they sent medicine, they sent letters and goodwill and hope, and here I am."

In an interview with Feminist.com, Loung spoke of her journey toward healing. She said:

> Each person's healing path is unique. Don't let other people hurry you, the path is different for everybody. I do believe, however, that it is not enough to go deep in your healing but you have to go wide as well. In the West, talk therapy often goes deep, but rarely are we ever told to go wide. When you go deep, you can get stuck in the thought that "this" is all

"With a global population of 6.3 billion people—that's a lot of potential for good to happen. If we all just do a little something, it'll go a long way. We need to realize that we are powerful beings. We live in a world where ordinary people do extraordinary things every day. They do not get the headlines, accolades, the awards. We don't know much about them but they're out there. They work miracles every day."
—Loung Ung

Ordinary people throughout Southeast Asia were drawn into the war. For the soldiers fighting, it was difficult to draw the line between civilians and enemies.

about you. But it's not. I survived the Khmer Rouge genocide—but so did 5 million other Cambodians; and 120 million others of other wars in the last century. What happened to me was not only a crime against Cambodians, but a crime against humanity. I have to keep this in mind, spread out the pain a little or I'll drown in it. So I get involved with causes, become an activist, and cast my nets for like-minded friends and helping hands everywhere. Because going deep without a safety line to pull you out when you're in the dark, you can get lost in it. It's important to keep a foot in the world as you are going inside your heart.

The average age of the American soldiers fighting in Vietnam was nineteen. This young man has put playing cards in his helmet for good luck.

DAN TODAY

Like Loung, Dan still has his share of nightmares—but like her, he's also learned to "keep a foot in the world." "I can never be the person I might have been," he said. "But this is what I got. I have to do what I can with it, use who I am for others."

After Dan came back from Vietnam, he lost job after job. He was in constant discomfort from shrapnel that had lodged in his back and hip. He took drugs to ease both his physical and emotional pain. After a few years, he ended up living on the street, eating at rescue missions, panhandling on the corner. "I didn't even recognize myself anymore. Who was this stinking, filthy guy? I didn't know. I was too blown away to care."

American soldiers search a Vietnamese village for enemies. Atrocities were committed on both sides during the war, leaving deep scars in the minds and hearts of those who survived.

A counselor started talking to Dan every day, and that made a difference. "Just being treated like a human being again . . . it made me start thinking. I started feeling like I *was* a human being, not just a sack of skin getting by on the street. I guess I was kind of like the Prodigal Son in the Bible. One day, I just thought, *I want to go home. I want to see my folks again.*"

For the next twelve years, Dan lived with his parents. Eventually, he went to college and got a degree in business management. "It took me nearly ten years to finish, but I made it. I couldn't have done it without my parents' patience. They put up with me when I wasn't easy to put up with.

Today, Loung Ung is a bestselling author and an activist who travels the world.

STEVEN D FRANCIS · HERBERT E FRENZELL · LARRY W GARDNER · EUGENE T GLOWACKI ·
JERRY F HOGAN · BILLY C JONES · WILLIAM A JONES Jr · GEORGE LOW ·
ROBERT E MATSON · HARRY J MILLER · EDGAR E NUSCHKE · HARDY W PEEPLES ·
LOUIS J WANDLER · JOHN L WILHELM · CHARLES M YATES · RAYMOND P ALBIETZ ·
DANIEL SANDUAL CASTILLO · WILLIE COLEMAN Jr · CLIFTON FREDERICK Jr · D C GEORGE ·
MELVIN T HUNTER · DAVID F KIES · RONALD L PENDERGIST · HAROLD W REYNOLDS ·

The names of
all the American
soldiers who
died during the
Vietnam War
are recorded
on the Wall in
Washington,
D.C., a
reminder to
all of us of the
immense cost
of war.

Vets With a Mission

Vietnam is no longer a nation torn apart by war—but the poor there still suffer from the effects of a war fought over three decades ago. According to the Vets With A Mission Web site, "A lack of basic health care knowledge and services in rural areas and poor districts of cities cause many to suffer from and to die of preventable diseases. Vets With A Mission has taken aggressive steps to educate the Vietnamese people about the dangers of poor health habits and to provide health care facilities and services for the disadvantaged. To date VWAM has built twenty-seven rural health care stations or small medical clinics in Viet Nam. . . . These rural health care stations and medical clinics in the cities established Vets With A Mission's long term commitment to providing health care for the people of Viet Nam."

They gave me a place to live when so many of my brothers were out on the street. They refused to give up on me."

Today, Dan works for an organization called Vets With A Mission (VWAM). VWAM provides health education and health-care facilities in Vietnam. "Success means something different to me today than it once did," Dan said. "I was going to run the farm, make money, have a good time. None of that happened. It just seems like a dream I once had, like something that was never real. For me, today, success means the ability to make a difference. I can never erase what the war did to me—or what I did during the war. All I have now is the present moment, today. I need to make use of it the best I can. I need to reach out to others."

PAST WARS

A Survivor of the Boer War

"I was at the camp today, and . . . a girl of twenty-one lay dying on a stretcher—the father, a big, gentle Boer, kneeling beside her, while in the next tent, his wife was watching a child of six, also dying, and one of five drooping. . . . For the most part, you must stand and look on, helpless, because there is nothing to do."
—Emily Hobhouse, 31 July 1901, South Africa

The Boer War was fought between Great Britain and the two Boer republics of Africa. The Boers were the white inhabitants of these republics who were mostly descended from early Dutch colonists.

Chapter Three

WAR IN EASTERN EUROPE

Have you ever heard the expression, "Wise beyond their years"? That's a good way to describe the people who have lived through the Yugoslav Wars. A middle-aged mother of two carries the same sad, weary expression as a young professional or an elderly grandmother. Their clothing styles may differ, their habits or interests may vary, but in the end, they all have one thing in common: they have lived through war.

DRAGANA'S STORY

"We were all friends before the war," Dragana, a Bosnian Serb, recalled. "The fact that they would bomb a multi-ethnic town was laughable. No one believed it." While ethnic tensions

From 1991 to 2001, the former Socialist Federal Republic of Yugoslavia (SFRY) endured a series of civil wars. Six republics make up the former nation of SFRY: Slovenia, Croatia, Bosnia Herzegovina, Montenegro, Macedonia, and Serbia. (Serbia is further broken down into two autonomous regions: Kosovo and Vojvodina.) While some territories endured more violence than others, not a single former Yugoslav republic was unaffected.

The two most gruesome and controversial of Yugoslav Wars were the Bosnian War and the Kosovo War. In the Bosnian War, the Serbs fought to extricate all Muslims from Bosnian territory to unify all territories where Serbs lived and create a "Greater Serbia." In the Kosovo War, the Serbs fought to extricate ethnic Albanians from Kosovo territory. Both wars involved a conflict of interests and led to examples of radical nationalism on the part of Serbia and what some deemed a form of "ethnic cleansing" by Serbian President Slobodan Milosevic.

ran rampart in Croatia, Serbia, and Kosovo, the common people of Bosnia seemed to live in relative peace with each other. Serbs, Croats, and Bosniaks befriended each other, just as Muslims were neighbors to Orthodox Christians, who were neighbors to Roman Catholics. Marriage between different ethnicities was common. The fact that Dragana was a Serb was a non-issue—until the fight for independence.

The majority of Bosnian Serbs did not support this independence, however, and, the Serbian government began an all-out attack

against Croats and Bosniaks, one of many acts of "ethnic cleansing" undertaken by Serbian President Milosevic during the Yugoslav Wars. Bosnian Serbs such as Dragana were suddenly looked upon as the enemy by people who had once been their friends and neighbors.

In 1993, Dragana had just given birth to her third child. As she lay in her hospital bed, she

The peaceful farmlands of what was known as Yogoslavia were devastated by war.

heard the rumble and crash of running feet as the Croatian army rushed into the hospital. Shouts filled the building; everyone had to evacuate immediately. Dragana was the only Serb in the hospital, and the other patients knew this; they sold her out to the Croatian soldiers. The soldiers were drunk and angry. Dragana's life was in danger, and so was her newborn son's.

"Go!" a doctor shouted to her. "And don't look back."

Shortly after Dragana escaped the hospital, the water and electricity went out all across town. "You knew something was going to happen, but not where or when. There was tension. I was anxious," Dragana said. The town had always been just a normal town, not dangerous at all, but a gut feeling told Dragana that she and her newborn son had to leave Bosnia immediately.

Dragana, her sister, and their children traveled by bus through the rainy darkness. They carried just two bags with them. But before they could cross the border out of Bosnia, the bus was stopped. The sisters were informed that no women or children were allowed to leave. Dragana felt trapped. "I wanted to go to free land," she said. "I didn't care where." Eventually, the family managed to travel to Kikinda, a small town in Serbia where Serbs were not in immediate danger.

Dragana and her family escaped unharmed except for a few scrapes and bruises. But many people she knew and loved were not

Opposite page: Most people of Eastern Europe are deeply religious. Muslims, Roman Catholics, and Orthodox live together. This shop sells Orthodox religious icons.

The land once known as Yugoslavia is an old one, where the past lives side by side with the present. It has endured through the centuries, but the violence of the twentieth century threatened to destroy its people.

so lucky. Bosnia was bombed after Dragana left. A children's school was the first target, and then a church. In a matter of days, the multi-ethnic republic of Bosnia became a war zone. Civilians who were not Serbian were slaughtered. Meanwhile, Bosnian Serbs were afraid that their neighbors would take revenge on them. "Bosnia became a military camp," Dragana said. "We got out, but a lot of family stayed and they were trapped."

Dragana fretted about the loved ones she left behind. The only contact she had with them was through Red Cross telegrams. For the next four years, her relatives moved from one abandoned house to another, in constant fear for their lives. Although none of her family members died in the bombing, her father was poisoned while in a Bosnian hospital; like many crimes that occurred in the chaos of the Yugoslav Wars, the death of Dragana's father was never investigated.

Meanwhile, Dragana and her immediate family had left everything behind them; she and her sister had to literally build their house in Kikinda from the floor up. The inflation rate was so high that instead of receiving money for work, Dragana and her family were paid a salary of nails, which they used to build their home.

Today, Dragana sits comfortably in the home she and her husband share. She smiles often and laughs. She is in her forties now, and fifteen years have passed since the day she fled Bosnia. Although she still has recurring dreams of hiding from the Croatian army, Dragana seldom thinks of the past during the day. Instead, she takes pride in all she has accomplished despite the war.

"I didn't think he would survive," she said, smiling at her teenage son, the one who was born on the eve of the war. "But now he is good in school and I am proud of my children."

"What difference does it make to the dead, the orphans and the homeless, whether the mad destruction is wrought under the name of totalitarianism or the holy name of liberty or democracy?"
—Mahatma Gandhi

Dragana and her husband somehow managed to raise a loving and happy family in the midst of war. She does not blame all Serbians for the actions of Serbian President Milosevic any more than she blames all Croats for the actions of a few drunken Croatian soldiers who forced her from the hospital fifteen years ago. "I knew Croatians who stole passports so that they wouldn't have to go to war," Dragana said. "I realize everyone is a victim, and our leaders are responsible."

Does she worry about her country's future? "I don't bother with tomorrow," she said and smiled.

VALERIA'S STORY

The Bosnian War was the conflict of Dragana's generation; the Kosovo War belonged to the next generation, to Valeria and her friends. Although they are over a decade apart in age, both Serbian women share a common expression. They have lived through war.

Now in her early thirties, Valeria will always connect being in her twenties with the sounds of war. "It is a strange thing to hear bombs outside," she said.

autonomous: self-governing, independent.

Kosovo was an **autonomous** region of Serbia, a land of great historical and religious importance to Serbians, although it's majority population consisted of ethnic Albanians.

repression: the state of being forcibly repressed, or kept down.

After years of **repression** from President Milosevic and the Serbian government, the ethnic Albanians of Kosovo demanded

Survivors of Other Wars: The Korean War

"They were skeletons—they were puppets of skin with sinews for strings—their faces were a terrible, translucent grey, and they cringed like dogs. They were manacled with chains or bound to each other with ropes. They were compelled to crouch in the classic oriental attitude of subjection, the squatting, fetal position, in heaps of garbage. . . . Finally, they were herded . . . into trucks with the numb air of men going to their deaths."

—James Cameron, journalist describing the treatment of South Korean prisoners, 1951

North Korea's war prisoners. The Korean War was a military conflict between North Korea (officially the Democratic People's Republic of Korea) and South Korea (officially the Republic of Korea) that lasted from 1950 until 1953. The conflict arose when the two Korean powers tried to re-unify Korea under their respective governments. The United States became involved in support of South Korea.

Today, the scars left by the war's bombs are still visible.

independence from Serbia; the Serbian government refused it. The Kosovo Albanians began with peaceful resistance, but in November 1997, frustration with the Serbian authorities eventually led to armed resistance and the formation of the **radical** Albanian group known as the Kosovo Liberation Army (KLA).

The KLA consisted mainly of farmers and unemployed ethnic Albanians who had grown sick and tired of Serbian repression. In the eyes of the Albanians, the KLA was a group of "freedom fighters." According to the Yugoslav government they resisted, the KLA were "terrorists." For over a year,

radical: one who supports fundamental and revolutionary changes in governments, societies, or practices.

Another bombed-out building is a reminder of the years of violence.

SANDVIČI

KIFLA:
NAMAZ, KAČKAVALJ,
NAMAZ, KAČKAVALJ,
NAMAZ, KAČKAVALJ,
RUSKA SALATA
PEČURKA SALATA
TUNJEVINA SALATA
PILEĆA SALATA
PONČO SALATA

EKSTRA DODAC
RUSKA SALATA
PEČURKA SALATA
TUNJEVINA SALATA
PILEĆA SALATA
KAJMAK
ŠUNKA
KULEN
PEČENICA
KAČKAVALJ

HOTDOG

PALAČIN

SLATKE:
DŽEM
EURO KREM
NUTELA

DODACI ZA PA

PLAZMA
LEŠNIK
ORAH
KOKOS
SUVO GROŽĐE
BANANE
VIŠNJA
ANANAS

Valeria today, as she stops at a street vendor to buy a snack.

the two groups fought constantly and many civilians died in the crossfire.

For every Serb the KLA murdered, the Serbs retaliated by murdering double or even triple the number of Kosovo Albanians. Secret executions, civilian murders, and massacres spread blood across the once peaceful communities. In October 1998, the North Atlantic Treaty Organization (NATO) troops entered Kosovo to restore order. After only a

Survivors of Other Wars: Algerian War of Independence

"Hundreds died when put to work clearing the minefields . . . or were shot out of hand. Others were tortured atrociously; army veterans were made to dig their own tombs, then swallow their decorations before being killed; they were burned alive . . . dragged behind trucks or cut to pieces. . . . Estimates of the numbers thus killed vary wildly between 30,000 and 150,000."

—Alistair Horne, describing Algeria's war for independence, 1962

Northern Africa and the Middle East

Algeria is in northern Africa. Once a French colony, in the 1960s it fought to gain its independence.

In these ordinary apartment buildings, Serbians continued to live their lives, despite the war.

few weeks, however, the ceasefire was lifted, and the violence resumed.

On January 15, 1999, the KLA attacked and killed a group of Serbian police in Kosovo. In retaliation, the Serbian police killed forty-five civilians in what would later be known as the Racak Massacre. NATO stepped in with an **ultimatum**: Serbia would either have to agree to sign peace accords and end the violence, or it would be bombed. Serbia refused. On March 24, 1999, with the support of former United States President Bill Clinton, NATO bombed Serbia.

ultimatum: a final demand or statement of terms that implies serious consequences if ignored.

The years of war have left Serbia struggling with poverty. Homelessness is common.

Valeria and
her younger
brother are
survivors who
still know how
to laugh.

"We heard the bombs outside as we were watching them on the television," Valeria remembered. "It was like watching a movie. It didn't feel real."

For those of us who have never witnessed war on our homeland's soil, the concept of being bombed or the thought of mass murders taking place in the community where we live seems unreal.

Survivors of Other Wars: Soviet Invasion of Afghanistan

"People mostly got killed either in their first month when they were too curious, or towards the end when they'd lost their sense of caution and become stupid. At night you'd forget where you were, who you were, what you were doing there. No one could sleep during the last six or eight weeks before they went home."

—Svetlana Alexiyevich, describing the Soviet Union's war in Afghanistan, 1990

Soviet tanks invading Afghanistan.

*The total death
toll for all
the Yugoslav
Wars is still
unknown.
Many of the
deaths were
carried out
in secret;
people simply
disappeared.
Hundreds of
thousands
were mur-
dered. Millions
were displaced.
Even to this
day, the death
toll rises as
people die on
the fields from
land mines
left over from
the wars. For
the people
of former
Yugoslavia,
the wars never
really ended
and the repub-
lics remain on
shaky ground.*

Modern Serbians carry on with their lives with the reminders of war all around them.

For us, war is something we see on television, not something that takes place in the streets of our hometowns. "You got used to it," Valeria explained. "It sounds funny to say you get used to explosions, but you do. Life goes on."

Rather than give in after the bombings began, the way NATO expected, Milosevic used the opportunity to expand his violence. While pointing a finger at the actions of NATO against Serbia, Milosevic and his secret police committed more acts of "ethnic cleansing" during the NATO bombings than at any other point during the Yugoslav Wars. Meanwhile, the bombings continued relentlessly for seventy-eight days. In the first week of NATO bombings, an estimated 300,000 Kosovo Albanians were forced to flee their homes. By April, that number had reached 850,000.

During the first few weeks and months of the bombing, many Serbians huddled inside their homes. As the bombing continued, though, some stopped being afraid. "For teenagers, the war had good things too," Valeria said. "School was closed. We would hang out with our friends and stay inside all day. We didn't really understand how awful it was. Our parents knew better. They were constantly scared."

infrastructure: the underlying framework or features of a system or organization.

Bridges were bombed, as well as factories and power plants. The destruction left Serbia's economy and **infrastructure** devastated. The Kosovo War finally came to an end on

Another Bosnian Survivor

"When you see me now, it is not as I really am. I am not this dirty, poor woman, in smelly clothes, that all my perfume cannot cover. I am not the person I was, you see . . . I never envied anyone before the war. And now I am consumed, eaten by envy. That's what I have been reduced to, what all of us have been reduced to in Bosnia. . . . We have become a nation of beggars.

"First I was a Yugoslav. Then I was a Bosnian. Now I'm becoming a Muslim. It's not my choice. I don't even believe in God. But after two hundred thousand dead, what do you want me to do?"

—Sarajevan woman, 1993

Bombed apartment buildings in a suburb of Sarajevo where Bosnian Serbs once lived.

Other War Survivors: World War I

"We'd only gone a hundred yards . . . when we encountered gas. We'd had no training . . . , never heard of the gas business. Our eyes were streaming with water and pain, and all we had was a roll of bandages in the first aid kit we carried in our tunic. So we bandaged each other's eyes, and anyone who could see would lead a line of half a dozen or so men, each with his hand on the shoulder of the man in front. In this way, lines and lines of British soldiers moved along, with rolls of bandages over their eyes."
—Sergeant Jack Dorgan, April 1915

A World War I soldier wears a bandage over his face to protect him from mustard gas.

June 11, 1999. In 2000, the Serbian government overthrew Milosevic, and six years later, he died awaiting trial for war crimes against humanity. On February 17, 2008, after years of fighting, Kosovo declared independence from Serbia.

Like Dragana, Valeria survived the horror of war—and like Dragana, today she is quick to smile. "If you did not laugh," she said, "you would cry."

The people of Bosnia and Serbia have lived through terrible violence. Today they face the future with both sadness and hope.

MIDDLE EAST

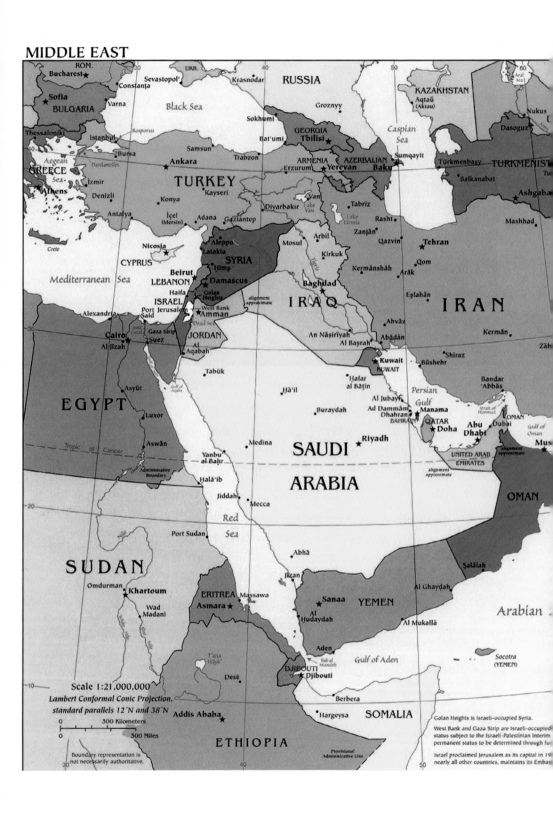

Chapter Four

WAR IN THE MIDDLE EAST

In Haifa Zangana's book *City of Widows*, the Iraqi author includes this story:

Baghdad is like a ghost city, most of its desperate 6.5 million inhabitants are imprisoned in their homes, it's simply too dangerous to venture out. After sunset hardly anyone leaves the house. Some people have between 15 minutes to 1 hour electricity per day supplied by the national grid; we were lucky enough to be able to afford a generator, but many people have to get through their days on this limited supply of electricity and at this time of year it's freezing cold in Baghdad and people have no way of heating their homes.

Seen through a night-vision device, U.S. paratroopers conduct a raid on a suspected terrorist's home in Iraq.

At night you hear the continual crackle of gunfire and rockets being launched. U.S. helicopters fly above the skies day and night, in some areas they fly very low, a few inches off the roofs of the houses so the house is constantly vibrating. As they fly above, U.S. soldiers drop heat-detecting objects to try and divide the missiles that are being fired in their direction by **insurgents**, fighters, militias, and whoever.

insurgents: those who are revolting against an established government.

There wasn't a minute in the day when I felt safe or secure; bullets are fired at houses by militia, and the U.S./ Iraqi military or militia can enter your house at anytime and arrest your son, brother, or father and you have very little idea if and when you might see them again.

One night a group of U.S. soldiers arrived at our house without any warning. They were trying to establish if we were militia and if we had guns. My elderly father-in-law pointed to the windows of the house where a few weeks ago armed militia had fired live rounds from a machine gun into the house; one of the bullets missed my sleeping sister-in-law's head by a few inches. The soldiers then asked my father-in-law if he wanted a gun and insisted that they would give him a weapon if he wanted one. He told them that all he wanted was for them to leave him and the family alone.

Zangana also includes the account of twelve-year-old Safa Younis:

The [soldiers] knocked at our front door and my father went to open it. They

"Everyone is shouting and bullets cut through the clouds of smoke and dust. What movie am I watching? Who killed the teenager on the bridge and why?

"Dead Iraqis litter the street. Shrapnel and concrete crunch underfoot as the Marines move house to house. An old gray-haired civilian lies slumped with his head rested against the steering wheel of his truck, he looks like my grandfather, except the back of his head is missing, he is covered with flies and bullet holes cover the windshield of his truck. I imagine his wife is waiting for him to return from work."

—Gary Knight, photographer who accompanied the U.S. Marines in Baghdad, 2004.

Scenes from the Iraq War.

shot him dead from behind the door and then they shot him again. They one American soldier came in and shot at us all. I pretended to be dead and he didn't notice me.

LAND OF OIL AND TENSION

Beginning in the 1970s, Saddam Hussein controlled Iraq. Under Saddam, Baghdad acquired training and weapons from the USSR, as well as economic protection for their valuable oil resources. But Saddam did not like the idea of relying too much on one foreign country for aid. Hoping to bring more diverse foreign interests into his country, Saddam began economic exchanges with Western countries, including France and Germany, making it clear Iraq wanted to act independently.

By this time, the United States and Britain were no friends to Iraq because Saddam had allied with their major enemy in the Middle East region, Iran. Meanwhile, Saddam was angry with the United States and Britain because of their support of Israel in the Palestinian conflict. Saddam had big plans for his country's success, starting with an invasion of Iran, his former ally.

In 1979, a radical Islamist government under the Ayatollah Khomeini came into power. The new Iranian government was equally threatening to Western and Eastern economic interests in the region, so when

"War may sometimes be a necessary evil. But no matter how necessary, it is always an evil, never a good. We will not learn how to live together in peace by killing each other's children."
—President Jimmy Carter

"Iraq is the 'cradle of civilization,' the home of Sumerian, Assyrian and Babylonian cultures and the birthplace of Abraham. The main Baghdad museum alone held more than 170,000 artifacts, including a vast treasury of cuneiform clay tablets that have yet to be translated. . . . No one yet knows what was pillaged from important museums in Mosul and Basra, which were also ransacked by looters. 'This is the crime of the century,' . . . a curator at the Baghdad museum told a summit of experts from the world's greatest museums. . . . The looted material belonged to all mankind.'"

—Fiachra Gibbons, journalist, on the Iraq War's destruction of cultural artifacts

Today, when people think of Iraq, they usually think of war. But Iraq is also the home to ancient archeological sites and museums that were once rich with history. This carving is from a king's door found in Iraq; it is nearly three thousand years old. Treasures like these have been lost forever to the war's destruction.

Iraq invaded Iran, most of the world's powerful nations threw their support behind Iraq, including the United States. America gave powerful technology, training, and weapons to Saddam Hussein.

Even so, the fighting between Iraq and Iran went on for eight long years, costing over a million people their lives. The United Nations did nothing to stop the bloodshed. Iraq and Iran were the chessboard where major nations **strategized** and watched.

strategized: planned; came up with strategies.

U.S. troops train Iraqi soldiers in a live-fire exercise.

Neither Western nor Eastern nations, however, could conduct business in the war-torn region, a region on which the world relied for its oil. Finally, in 1988, the United States and the Soviet Union worked together to make a UN peace agreement for Iraq and Iran, and the war ended.

The eight-year war with Iran had cost Iraq billions of dollars, and Saddam

Captured by U.S. forces on December 13, 2003, Saddam was brought to trial under the Iraqi interim government set up by U.S.-led forces. On November 5, 2006, he was convicted of charges related to the executions of 148 Iraqis, and he was sentenced to death by hanging. Saddam was executed on December 30, 2006.

was looking to **recoup** his losses, so in 1990, he decided to invade Kuwait, a small country with 10 percent of the world's oil, a virtual treasure trove of wealth. Saddam failed to realize that most of the world's nations opposed his actions; if Kuwait belonged to Iraq, the rest of the world would have less access to the tiny country's rich resources. A coalition of thirty-four nations, including the United States, mounted a counterattack against Iraq. The coalition was victorious, and **sanctions** were placed on Iraq that were intended to rein in Saddam for the next decade.

After the terrorist attacks of September 11, 2001, the U.S. government turned suspicious eyes on Saddam. Some political advisors indicated that Saddam was sheltering Osama bin Laden, who was responsible for the 9/11 attacks. Many Americans believed the Iraq government under Saddam Hussein was hiding weapons of mass destruction. The U.S. government **ousted** Saddam, and it insisted that military occupation would bring freedom and democracy to Iraq.

Political analysts disagree on the effectiveness of the Iraq war, but one thing is certain: like any war, it has been violent and brutal—and it has left deep scars in all those who have survived it, both Americans and Iraqi. For the soldiers fighting the war, as in the Vietnam War, the lines between enemy and civilian are often difficult to see. The three stories that follow, told by American soldiers

recoup: regain, recover, get back the equivalent of.

sanctions: penalties imposed as a consequence of ignoring or violating international law.

ousted: forced out.

to journalist Emilie DePrang, show how ugly war is.

MICHAEL'S STORY

One night they said to me, "Sergeant Goss, gather your best guys." I say, "Where we going?" They say, "Don't worry about it, just come on." So we get in the car and go. We drive three blocks away, and there's six dead soldiers on the ground. They say, "You're casualty collecting tonight." I'm not prepared for that. I wasn't taught how to do that. But you're there. So you pick them up, and you put them in a body bag, pieces by pieces, and you go back to your unit, and you stand inside your room. And they're like, "You're going on a patrol, come on." You're like, "Hang on a minute. Let me think about what I just did here." I just put six American guys in . . . body bags. Nobody's prepared for that. Nobody's prepared for that thing to blow up on the side of the road. You're talking, and you're driving, and then something blows up, and the next thing you know, two of your guys are missing their faces. They just want you to get up the next day and go, go, let's do it again, you're a soldier. . . .

It gets to the point where they numb you. They numb you to death. They numb you to anything. You come back, and it starts coming back to you slowly. Now you gotta figure out a way to deal with it. In Iraq you had a way to deal with it, because they kept

Opposite page: Each of these white flags on the University of Oregon's campus symbolizes six Iraqis who have died in the war; nearly a million Iraqi civilians have died since the war began.

pushing you back out there. Keep pushing you back out into the streets. Go, go, go. Hey, I just shot four people today. Yeah, and in about four hours you're going to go back out, and you'll probably shoot six more. So let's go. Just deal with it. We'll fix it when we get back. That's basically what they're telling you. We'll fix it all when we get back. We'll get your head right and everything when we get back to the States. I'm sorry, it's not like that. It's not supposed to be like that. All the soldiers have post-traumatic stress disorder. . . .

I have PTSD. I know when I got it—the night I killed an eight-year-old girl. Her family was trying to cross a checkpoint. We'd just shot three guys who'd tried to run a checkpoint. And during that mess, they were just trying to get through to get away from it all. And we ended up shooting all them, too. It was a family of six. The only one that survived was a thirteen-month-old and her mother. And the worst part about it all was that where I shot my bullets, when I went to see what I'd shot at, there was an eight-year-old girl there. I tried my best to bring her back to life, but there was no use.

ROCKY'S STORY

I was one of those kids that could have been handed anything on a silver platter. But I really worked hard for everything anyway, because I wanted to prove myself. And my parents, who would have given me anything, ruled with an iron fist. And I was patriotic. So it seemed like everything in my life pointed to the Army as the way to go.

I was twenty. I'm sure I was different then. I don't know how. I know how I am now. I assume that the character traits that I show now are the core set of values that I left with. My sense of pride, hard work. Everything I have, I made out of nothing.

U.S. forces in Iraq.

A U.S. soldier on patrol pauses to offer gum to local children.

You get to see what people are made of over there. You get to see how shallow people are, how weak they are. How strong they can be in horrible moments. And then how the people you should be looking up to are

According to a study published in the New England Journal of Medicine in 2004, 86 percent of soldiers in Iraq reported knowing someone who was seriously injured or killed there. Some 77 percent reported shooting at the enemy; 75 percent reported seeing women or children in imminent peril and being unable to help. Fifty-one percent reported handling or uncovering human remains; 28 percent were responsible for the death of a noncombatant. One in five Iraq veterans return home seriously impaired by post-traumatic stress disorder.

hiding, and you have to look out for them. You get to really see what a person is made of.

And over there, I learned to read people. I know what they're going to do before they do it. After seeing the same movements before you get shot at or bombed, the same symptoms of the city and the people around you—it's a fluid movement. Doors close, people disappear, and all of a sudden you're like, OK guys, hunker down, it's about to hit us. And all of a sudden, you're under fire.

People would pop shots at us and pop back. They'd have a setup where they have a bomb in the road, and everybody sits by the windows when they set [it] off. . . . When we're looking at what's going on, every-body's laughing and pointing and smiling after your buddy's sitting there bleeding. So I held them all responsible. Everybody that was in the guilty range.

If there was gunfire coming from a window, I shot into that window and made sure nothing was coming back out at me. One time, there was . . .a shooter shooting at me. . . . He hit the **Bradley** in front of us, and the round didn't go off. It got stuck in the mud. So the Bradley rolled back, and we rolled back. And I had to shoot the position-caller before I could shoot the actual shooter. He didn't have a gun, but I knew what he was doing. He was the one calling out what's going on. He was on the phone. So I sent a shot up twenty feet above him and below him and to the side of him. And he just stood there. On his phone, talking the whole time. Innocent people run. The bad guys stay and fight. If they're not running, they're going to be calling. That's the way I see it. So I shot him. If you freaked out and stood still, I'm sorry. I cannot take this chance again. . . .

After that, now I think, well, now . . . I've done the worst thing. There's not much more worse you can do than shoot an unarmed person. . . . You feel so horrible. You kind of die inside. There's really nothing beneath me now. I'm at the bottom of the barrel. You're worried about salvation and people finding out these dirty little secrets. It's not something that you wanted to do. It might be something that you had to do, that you accidentally did. Things happen. And then there's the whole fear of going to jail for trying to do what's right for your country—it's bad. Sometimes you think people are shooting at you, and

Bradley:
short for the Bradley Fighting Vehicle, a 25-ton armored personnel carrier named by World War II general Omar Bradley.

"We have fought during fifteen days for a single house. . . . Faces black with sweat, we bombard each other with grenades in the middle of explosions, clouds of dust and smoke, heaps of mortar, floods of blood, fragments of furniture and human beings. . . . The street is no longer measured by meters but by corpses. . . . Stalingrad is no longer a town. . . . When night arrives, one of those scorching, howling, bleeding nights, the dogs plunge into the [river] and swim desperately to gain the other bank. The nights of Stalingrad are a terror for them. Animals flee this hell . . . only men endure."

—a Panzer officer, World War II Battle of Stalingrad, 1943

Soldiers fighting in the rubble that was once Stalingrad. The experiences described by an officer during World War II's Battle of Stalingrad are not so different from those of American soldiers fighting in Baghdad.

"I saw the flash of light. . . . Not only my present but also my past and future were blown away in the blast. My beloved students burned together in a ball of fire right before my eyes. Then I collected my wife . . . who had now become a bucket-full of soft ashes, from the burnt-out ruin of our house. She had died in the kitchen."

—Dr. Takasha Nagai, survivor of Nagasaki, 1945

The mushroom cloud over Nagasaki after the atom bomb was dropped on it during World War II.

you'd rather just chance it because you're hoping they don't have an armor-piercing round.

. . . . I try to do right now. I don't want to hurt anybody's feelings. I go to school, maybe I'll earn a midlevel job. Just fly under the radar. I don't want any attention. I just want to be away from people. Not many people call me still. I keep it real dim in my apartment. I like it calm and quiet. This is what life's made of. Being able to relax and be safe. Watch a movie, play some video games. Just to sit back and have fun with your friends. That's beautiful.

SUE'S STORY

I joined the Army because I had $65,000 in student loans and didn't know how I was going to make payments. Since I had a master's in political science—Middle East studies and Arabic—I ended up doing translation as part of the search for weapons of mass destruction. For a year, my team drove around behind the 3rd Infantry getting shot at, getting mortared, looking at warehouses of documents, chemicals, and parts of things that could be weapons of mass destruction. I mean, you name it, we did it. We talked to people. We went into people's houses.

The technological level of the things I saw wasn't anywhere near anything [former Secretary of State] Colin Powell talked about. The buildings we went into, wiring was on

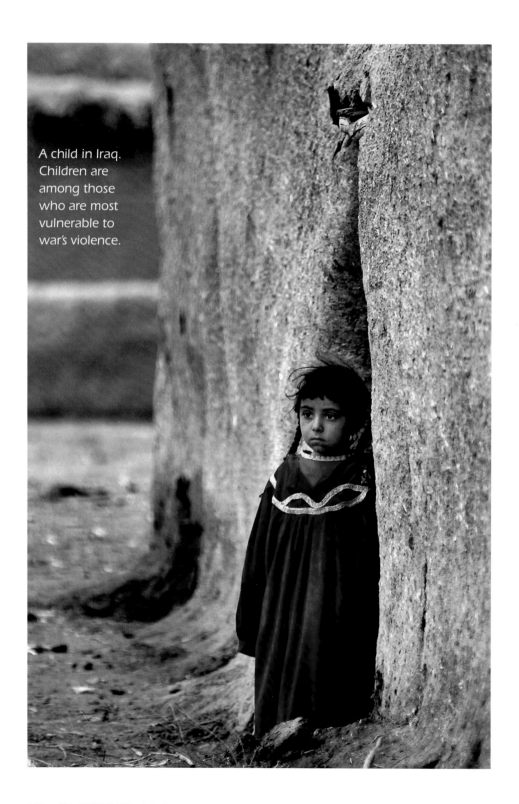

A child in Iraq. Children are among those who are most vulnerable to war's violence.

the outside of the walls. I didn't see anything like the equipment you'd see in a fifth-grade science lab. The most technically advanced thing we saw was a 12-volt car battery hooked up to bedsprings for torture. But not anything on the chemical or biological level.

Iraq looks like it's straight out of the Bible. It's mud brick, it's falling down. It's kids with sticks herding goats. There's like three high-rises in all of Baghdad, and those are the only ones you'll ever see on any newscast. The rest of it is mud brick falling down.

At the time, I would see little girls on the side of the road, and I felt like I was part of a big machine that was going to help them have a better life. . . . [But] when I went back to my base in Germany, it was like a bad dream. It was like nothing happened. Then I got out of the Army and came back to the States. Once you leave the Army, there's no reintegration help of any kind. Unless you went looking for it, there was nothing. And even if you went looking for it, you had to dig.

The military says that they're giving exit counseling and reintegration. What they're

"I have seen war. I have seen war on land and sea. I have seen blood running from the wounded. I have seen the dead in the mud. I have seen cities destroyed. I have seen children starving. I have seen the agony of mothers and wives. I hate war."
—President Franklin Delano Roosevelt

"We talked the matter over and could have settled the war in thirty minutes had it been left to us."

—a Rebel soldier made this statement after talking with a Union soldier across the lines during the American Civil War

calling reentry counseling, in my experience, was, "Don't drink and drive. Pay your bills on time. Don't beat your spouse. Don't kick your dog." All of these things that once you've reached a certain age, you're supposed to know. None of it is, "If you have discomfort with dealing with crowds, if you don't feel comfortable with your spouse, if you can't sleep in a bed, if you don't want to drive down the road because you think everything is a bomb, here's what to do." . . .

They don't prepare you to leave . . . they didn't prepare me to be there. I was going into people's houses trying to tell the wife and kids as we're segregating them out from the men that we're the good guys. But they're crying because one of their kids got killed because he was up there sleeping on the roof when we decided to bust into their house. I mean that's crazy. But we're the good guys. Now I have to deal with that for the next twenty or thirty years. I have a three-year-old. I deal with that every day.

I think we are going to end up like after Vietnam if we're not careful. The Vietnam guys were treated really horribly, and whether they came back and quietly went back to their lives or not, they were all **stereotyped** in a criminal negative. And I'm afraid if we as a society don't learn what we didn't do for those guys, we're going to have that in spades. We don't have low-end kind of industry jobs for them like working in the auto plant, so they're not going to be sup-

stereotyped: used a standard and oversimplified idea or image often used to describe a group or members of a group.

Two Sides of the Story

According to the International Committee of the Red Cross (ICRC) raids by American soldiers on Iraqis often looked like this:

> Arresting authorities entered houses usually after dark, breaking down doors, waking up residents roughly, yelling orders, forcing family members into one room under military guard while searching the rest of the house and further breaking doors. cabinets, and other property. They arrested suspects, tying their hands in the back with flexicuffs, hooding them, and taking them away. Sometimes they arrested all adult males in the house, including elderly, handicapped, or sick people. Treatment often included pushing people around, insulting, taking aim with rifles, punching and kicking, and striking with rifles. Individuals were often led away in whatever they happened to be wearing at the time of arrest—sometimes pajamas or underwear. . . . In many cases personal belongings were seized during the arrest with no receipt given. . . . In almost all incidents documented by the ICRC, arresting authorities provided no information about who they were, where their base was located, nor did they explain the cause of arrest. Similarly, they rarely informed the arrestee or his family where he was being taken or for how long, resulting in the de facto disappearance of the arrestee for weeks or even months until contact was finally made.

However, Major John Dunlap, the chief law investigator for American troops, believes that American soldiers in Iraq have no choice. He said in an interview with NPR:

> Soldiers were called upon to make decisions on a daily basis in snap seconds. And we did not want to create an environment where soldiers thought they were going to be second-guessed and prosecuted for making decisions that would save their life. Rule number one is to come home alive.

porting their families. . . . I don't know how. But there isn't enough money in this country right now to make some of these guys feel like what they went through was worthwhile.

We have no comprehension of the psychological cost of this war. I know kids in Iraq who killed themselves. I know kids that got killed. OK, that's apparently the price of

A Survivor of the Spanish Civil War

"Fire enveloped the whole city. Screams of lamentation were heard everywhere and the people, filled with terror, knelt, lifting their hands to heaven as if to implore divine protection. . . . The first hours of the night presented a terrible spectacle of men and women in the woods outside the city searching for their families and friends. Most of the corpses were riddled with bullets."
—the Dean of Valladoid Cathedral, April 1937

These children were left as refugees during the Spanish Civil War.

Survivors of the Russian Civil War were left wounded and traumatized.

doing business. But multiply me by 2 million. If I'm fairly high-functioning, what about the ones that aren't? They're going back to small-town America, and their families aren't going to know what to do with them.

WARS AND THE HUMAN RACE

Human beings have been fighting wars since before the dawn of history. The reasons for wars are still the same as ever: religion, land, resources. Sometimes war seems to be inevitable—but it is also terrible. It costs human

Survivors of military conflicts know that peace is precious, a goal worth working toward.

lives—and the survivors are left with scars they will bear forever.

President Dwight Eisenhower said:

Every gun that is made, every warship launched, every rocket fired signifies in the final sense, a theft from those who hunger and are not fed, those who are cold and are not clothed. This world in arms is not spending money alone. It is spending the sweat of its laborers, the genius of its scientists, the hopes of its children. This is not a way of life at all in any true sense. Under the clouds of war, it is humanity hanging on a cross of iron.

Further Reading

Buzzell, Colby. *My War: Killing Time in Iraq.* New York: Putnam, 2005.

Crawford, John. *The Last True Story I'll Ever Tell: An Accidental Soldier's Account of the War in Iraq.* New York: Riverhead, 2005.

Hatzfeld, Jean. *Life Laid Bare: The Survivors in Rwanda Speak.* Linda Coverdale, trans. New York, N.Y.: Other Press, 2006.

———. *Machete Season: The Killers in Rwanda Speak.* Linda Coverdale, trans. New York, N.Y.: Farrar, Straus and Giroux, 2005.

Ung, Loung. *First They Killed My Father: A Daughter of Cambodia Remembers.* New York: Harper Perennial, 2001.

Zangana, Haifa. *City of Widows: An Iraq Woman's Account of War and Resistance.* New York: Seven Stories, 2007.

For More Information

Cambodian Genocide Program
Yale University
www.yale.edu/cgp

Center for Balkan Development
www.friendsofbosnia.org/index.html

Genocide in Rwanda
www.unitedhumanrights.org/Genocide/
genocide_in_rwanda.htm

Immaculée Ilibagiza.
www.immaculee.com

Vets with a Mission
www.vwam.com/vets/nprojects.html

The Vietnam War: America's Longest War
www.vietnamwar.com

War in Iraq
Special Reports from CNN
www.cnn.com/SPECIALS/2003/iraq

Publisher's note:
The Web sites listed on this page were active at the time of publication. The publisher is not responsible for Web sites that have changed their addresses or discontinued operation since the date of publication. The publisher will review and update the Web-site list upon each reprint.

Bibliography

Benson, Leslie. *Yugoslavia: A Concise History.* Hampshire, U.K.: Palgrave, 2001.

Clymer, Kenton. *The United States and Cambodia, 1969–2000: A Troubled Relationship.* New York: Routledge, 2004.

DePrang, Emilie. "Iraq Comes Home: Soldiers Share the Devastating Tales of War." Information Liberation, July 24, 2007. www.informationliberation.com/?id=22882.

"Genocide Survivor Can't Forgive." BBC News. April 7, 2006. news.bbc.co.uk/2/hi/africa/4877212.stm.

Haas, Michael. *Cambodia, Pol Pot, and the United States: the Faustian Pact.* New York: Praeger, 1991.

———. *Genocide by Proxy: Cambodian Pawn on a Superpower Chessboard.* New York: Praeger, 1991.

Hatzfeld, Jean. *Life Laid Bare: The Survivors in Rwanda Speak.* Linda Coverdale, trans. New York: Other Press, 2006.

Hatzfeld, Jean. *Machete Season: The Killers in Rwanda Speak.* Linda Coverdale, trans. New York: Farrar, Straus and Giroux, 2005.

Immaculée Ilibagiza. www.immaculee.com.

Judah, Tim. *The Serbs: History, Myth and the Deconstruction of Yugoslavia*. 2nd ed. New Haven, Conn.: Yale Nota Bene, 2000.

Knightly, Phillip. *The Eye of War*. Washington, D.C.: Smithsonian, 2003.

Library of Congress: Federal Research Division. "A Country Study: Yugoslavia (former)." lcweb2.loc.gov/frd/cs/yutoc.html.

Ljubisic, Davorka. *A Politics of Sorrow: The Disintegration of Yugoslavia*. Montreal, Calif.: Black Rose Books, 2004.

Rucyahana, John, and James Riordan. *The Bishop of Rwanda: Finding Forgiveness Amidst a Pile of Bones*. Nashville, Tenn.: Thomas Nelson, 2007.

"Rwandan Genocide Survivor Recalls Horror, Hid in Tiny Bathroom for Three Months with Six Other Women." 60 Minutes. July 1, 2007. www.cbsnews.com/stories/2006/11/30/60minutes/main2218371.shtml.

Schnall, Marianne. "Conversation with Loung Ung." Feminist.com. www.feminist.com/resources/artspeech/interviews/loungung.html.

"Tears and Smiles in the Fight for Justice: Five Victims of Human Rights Violations on How They are Now Fighting for Human Rights in

Bibliography

Their Countries." *The Observer*. Sept. 21, 2008. www.guardian.co.uk/world/2008/sep/21/humanrights1.

"Twenty-Five Lectures on Modern Balkan History," www.lib.msu.edu/sowards/balkan/.

Walter, Sara. "Survivor Recounts Rwandan Genocide." *Brown Daily Herald*. 10/19/05. media.www.browndailyherald.com/media/storage/paper472/news/2005/10/19/CampusNews/Survivor.Recounts.Rwandan.Genocide-1025573.shtml.

Zangana, Haifa. *City of Widows: An Iraq Woman's Account of War and Resistance*. New York: Seven Stories, 2007.

Zograf, Aleksandar. *Bulletins from Serbia*. Hove, U.K.: Slab-O-Concrete Publications, 1999.

Index

activist 55, 61, 63
army 50, 72, 75, 81, 105, 111, 113
    Kosovo Liberation Army (KLA) 79, 80, 83
arrests 95, 115
assassination 13, 15

bin Laden, Osama 101
bomb 51, 57, 69, 74, 75, 76, 78, 79, 83, 85, 88, 89, 107, 109, 110, 114

civilian 12, 15, 51, 57, 60, 74, 80, 83, 96, 101, 103
concentration camp 58
conflict 9, 13, 50, 53, 70, 76, 77, 97, 118
corruption 11, 40
coup 11
criminal 28, 114

defense 11, 12, 32
democracy 75, 101
draft 52

economic 24, 88, 97
ethnic 11, 13, 45, 69, 70, 74, 76, 79
    ethnic cleansing 70, 71, 88
execution 38, 80, 100
extremists 15

forgiveness 25, 36, 37, 39, 40, 42

genocide 16, 17, 22, 24–27, 29, 31, 32, 34, 36, 40, 61
    Rwanda 9–45
government 11, 45, 47, 51, 53, 70, 76, 77, 79, 91, 95, 97, 100, 101

gunfire 94, 108

helicopter 94
history 11, 44, 53, 98, 117
Hussein, Saddam 97, 99, 100, 101

independence 13, 53, 70, 79, 81, 91
industry 114
insurgent 95

machetes 9, 16, 19, 20, 23, 27, 28, 29, 32, 34
massacre 16, 19, 25, 27, 83
military 11, 12, 15, 48, 50, 53, 56, 74, 77, 95, 101, 113, 115, 118
militias 15, 95
murder 19, 25, 32, 80, 85, 86
mustard gas 90

nationalism 70
North Atlantic Treaty Organization (NATO) 81, 83, 88

patriotic 19, 105
peace 12, 24–26, 34, 40, 54, 56, 59, 70, 71, 79, 81, 83, 97, 100, 114, 118
politics 11, 12, 101, 111
population 30, 48, 59, 76
post-traumatic stress disorder 55, 104, 107
president 15, 16, 70, 71, 76, 83, 97, 113, 119

radical 70, 79, 97
Red Cross 75, 115
refugees 20, 116
religion 72, 76, 117

Index

Picture Credits

Archives of Ontario: p. 116

CIA: pp. 46, 68, 92

Creative Commons
Attribution ShareAlike 2.0
Generic
    Klika, Russell Lee: p. 112

Dreamstime Photo
    Chaikovsky: p. 24
    Cherry, Brian: pp. 105,
        106
    Ellegon: p. 22
    Howard, Lori: p. 102
    Zambiamdeve: p. 8

Harding House Publishing
    Stewart, Benjamin: pp.
        71, 72, 74, 78, 79,
        80, 82, 83, 84, 87, 91

Harry S. Truman Library:
p. 77

iStockphoto
    Chesbrough, Jordan: p.
        17

Churchill, Robert: p. 54
Guni, Guenter: pp. 21,
    26, 30
Lyngfjel, Geir-olav: pp.
    64–65
Parekh, Shayna: p. 10
Pargeter, Kirsty: p. 118
Pomortzeff: p. 49
VonBuskirk, Jamie: p.
    52
Warren, Jason R.: p. 18

Jastrow: p. 98
Ung, Loung: p. 63

United States Department
of Defense: pp. 94, 99

United States Federal
Government: pp. 85, 89, 96

United States National
Archives: pp. 14, 44, 56, 60,
61, 62

To the best knowledge of the publisher, all images not specifically credited are in the public domain. If any image has been inadvertently uncredited, please notify Harding House Publishing Service, 220 Front Street, Vestal, New York 13850, so that credit can be given in future printings.

About the Author and the Consultant

Author

Sheila Stewart has written over two dozen educational books for young people. She lives in Western New York with her family.

Joyce Zoldak lives in New York City and works for the nonprofit sector. She will be pursuing a master's degree in Urban Policy in fall 2009.

Consultant

Andrew M. Kleiman, M.D. is a Clinical Instructor in Psychiatry at New York University School of Medicine. He received a BA in philosophy from the University of Michigan, and graduated from Tulane University School of Medicine. Dr. Kleiman completed his internship, residency, and fellowship in psychiatry at New York University and Bellevue Hospital. He is currently in private practice in Manhattan and teaches at New York University School of Medicine.